THE PEACE OF GOD

GENUINE PEACE FOR TURBULENT TIMES

Linda P. Jones

The Peace of God

By Linda P. Jones

Copyright ©2017 by Linda P. Jones

All rights reserved

No portion of this book may be reproduced, stored in a retrieval system, or transmitted in any form or by any means - electronic, mechanical, photocopy, recording, scanning or any other - except for brief quotations in critical reviews or articles, without the prior written permission of the author except as provided by USA copyright laws.

Unless otherwise noted, all Scripture quotations from the Holy Bible, are taken from the New King James Version and King James Versions of the

Holy Bible © 1979, 1980, 1982 by Thomas Nelson Inc.

Cover Design Andre Trotman - Bluestrip Design Studio
Editing by Paula Richards - Eagle's Eye Editing Services

CreateSpace

First printing, 2017

ISBN-13: 978-1977910622

ISBN-10: 1977910629

Contents

Introduction iii

The Peace of God is a Present 1

The Peace of God is a Resident 3

The Peace of God is Present 5

The Peace of God is Different 7

The Peace of God is Constant and Permanent 9

The Peace of God is Transcendent 11

The Peace of God has an Agreement 13

The Peace of God is Vigilant 15

The Peace of God is An Interagent 17

The Peace of God is Abundant 19

The God of Peace is Militant Part 1 21

The God of Peace is Militant Part 2 23

The Peace of God is Militant Part 3 25

The Peace of God is His Judgment in our Favor 27

The Peace of God is His Announcement to the World 29

The Call to Be Peacemakers 31

About the Author 33

Introduction

When we think of peace, we always think it's an absence of war or turmoil. 'When everything goes right in my life then I will have peace', we think. Such a peace is transient. Today men's hearts are failing them for fear as the Bible said would happen, and you read or hear of more wars and rumors of wars almost every week. People are desperate for peace and are seeking it here, there and everywhere. Those who could afford it take vacations and travel the world in hope of finding peace; some go to quiet places, others climb mountains to be close to nature, others move away from mainstream society to live in remote places, all in hope of finding peace. No doubt one will find a measure of tranquillity in some of these places. Then there are those who try to find some kind of peace from the use of alcohol, drugs, immorality, money, status, position. But true peace, genuine and lasting peace, is not found in a thing, place or activity; it is ultimately found in a Person - the Person of Jesus Christ.

Allow me to share with you some of the things I learnt about the peace of God during a recent time of difficulty.

The Peace of God is a Present - It is a Gift

How do you react when someone gives you a gift? If you are like me, you are thankful and very excited to open the package to discover what's inside. When Jesus said, *"Peace I leave with you, My peace I give to you"*-John 14:27, He was offering us His peace as a present. In John chapter 14, Jesus spoke to His disciples about His imminent departure from them and from earth, and was comforting them and assuring them that though He was leaving them physically He was leaving them with the indispensable gift of His Peace, which He knew they would need in the days to come days and for their lives here on earth as a whole. This is the same peace Jesus bequeaths to us as His present - His Gift. We so desperately need it in these troubled times. Will you receive His gift?

The Peace of God is a Resident

Peace is the condition of a heart reconciled to God through Christ. *"Therefore, having been justified by faith, we have peace with God through our Lord Jesus Christ"* –Romans 5:1. When a man is reconciled to God by accepting Jesus Christ as his Savior, then peace comes to reside inside of him. As a resident, the peace of God comes to stay to dwell, to inhabit and to occupy our lives. 2 Corinthians 13:11 states, *"Finally, brethren, farewell. Become complete. Be of good comfort, be of one mind, live in peace; and the God of love and peace will be with you".* Romans 15:33, *"Now the God of peace be with you all. Amen."* There are many other verses that speak of the peace of God being with you. The peace God gives is meant to stay, to never leave you. Actually, when Jesus said *"My peace I leave you",* He was declaring that He left His peace to us as a lasting legacy. However, the only way peace will not stay or dwell with us is if we constantly entertain worry, fears, doubts and sin - these are definite enemies of peace.

Wouldn't you like the peace of God to be a tenant or resident in you? I sure would.

The Peace of God is Present

'Present' is a noun but also an adjective. As an adjective it means 'it is at hand', 'it is there', 'available'. In my days at school, every day the teacher would take roll call. He/she would call every child's name that was supposed to be in class, and when your name was called, you would put up your hand and answer 'present' or 'here,' and a tick would be placed next to your name on the records to show that you were in attendance that day at school. That is how God's peace is – it is present, it is at hand, it is nearby, you don't have to wonder if it will be there for you. You don't have to go anywhere to get it; it is yours to have at no cost. Jesus said my peace I leave with you and He is not an Indian giver; He won't take it back.

The Peace of God is Different

Jesus said, *"Peace I leave with you, My peace I give to you; not as the world gives do I give to you. Let not your heart be troubled, neither let it be afraid"* –John 14:27. He specified that it was His peace as opposed to the peace the world gives you; it is distinctive. The peace of the world is fickle and fleeting. It's the kind of peace that is dependent on circumstances being just right – like having enough money in the bank to pay the bills, or everyone in the family gets along, or having food in the cupboard, or there is no war or threats of war. The peace the world gives is a peace that works when everything is going well, which it rarely does, and if it does it is only for a short time. Jesus' peace is very different from the pseudo-peace the world offers. And as we go along we will see how it is different.

We want to stop here and thank God for His peace, it is His special gift to you.

The Peace of God is Constant and Permanent

Apostle Paul blessed the believers in the Thessalonian church with this benediction, *"Now may the Lord of peace Himself give you peace always in every way. The Lord be with you all"* –2 Thessalonians 3:16. As we said earlier, the peace of this world is short lived, but the peace God gives is permanent. The Amplified Bible puts the verse this way, *"Now may the Lord of peace Himself grant you His peace (the peace of His kingdom) at all times and in all ways [under all circumstances and conditions, whatever comes]. The Lord [be] with you all."* In this world of momentary pleasures and continuous changes, absolutely nothing can be guaranteed to be constant outside of Christ Himself. In such a world it is good to know that the peace of God will not get up and leave you. It is constant under all circumstances and conditions, regardless of what comes your way. Friends come and friends go, but God's peace is constant and permanent. That is comforting.

This is the peace He offers to those who would come to Him through His Son Jesus Christ.

The Peace of God is Transcendent

"And the peace of God which passes all understanding" –Philippians 4:7. The word 'transcend' means 'to go beyond the limit, to rise above, exceed, to surpass.' We already established that this peace is far superior to the world's peace, but it is also superior to our finite thinking and understanding. It is the peace that does not make sense, so to speak. It is the peace you have in the face of chaos, when everything around you is chaotic – when the children are acting crazy, your husband is even crazier or your marriage is on the verge of a breakdown. It is the peace that causes you to stand when the doctor gives you a very negative report on your health or your loved one. It is the peace that enables you to leave stay calm his office which baffles him. You should be crying, worried, frantic, having a meltdown, but instead the peace of God rises above, transcends your understanding and takes pre-eminence. This is the peace that God gives – it is overwhelming and supreme to our

reasoning, which would say 'you ought to lose your mind.'

Today, let the peace of God fill your very being and transcend every chaotic situation in your life today. Not only does the peace of God transcend all understanding, but I like to say it transcends all misunderstanding as well. When you are misunderstood, God will give you a peace that rises above that and settles your heart.

The Peace of God has an Agreement

Yes, it will transcend all understanding but the prerequisite is well stated in the Amplified version –Philippians 4:6, *"Do not fret or have any anxiety about anything, but in every circumstance and in everything, by prayer and petition (definite requests), with thanksgiving, continue to make your wants known to God.* Verse 7 says *"And the peace of God which surpasses, all understanding, will keep your hearts and mind through Christ Jesus."* The agreement for peace is this – rather than be fretful and anxious, make your requests to God with continuous prayer and thanksgiving, and the promise is, that God's surpassing peace will keep your heart and mind through Christ. Isaiah 26:3 the corresponding Old Testament verse states, *"You will keep him in perfect peace whose mind is stayed on You."* The word 'stayed' means 'to lean, lay, rest, support, put, to lean upon.' When you let your mind lean on, rest on the Lord, not just peace, but perfect peace will be yours

Recently, something happened to me that severely threatened my peace of mind. At times I thought I was going to go crazy, but minute by minute I would make deliberate, conscious decisions to think on the Lord; to keep my mind on Him in order to make it through. And God's peace did keep my mind, it preserved and it guarded me, and He will do the same for you regardless of the circumstances.

The Peace of God is Vigilant

It is a peace that *"will keep (or guard) your hearts and minds through Christ Jesus"* – Philippians 4:7. The word *'keep'* means to act as a garrison. A garrison is a body of troops stationed in a fort or military post to defend it against an enemy, or to keep the inhabitants in subjection. A garrison is also a fort, castle or fortified town, furnished with troops to defend it. This reminds me of movies I've watched where the American army was at war with the Native American Indians. The army would build these supposedly impregnable forts and soldiers would be stationed on the walls all around on 24-hour lookout for the enemy. And that's the picture here of what the peace of God will do and be. It will be like a fortified town. It will be as a body of troops stationed on guard 24-7, watchful to defend our hearts and minds from intrusion by the enemy. Peace will be vigilant to watch and to guard our hearts from fear, depression and anxiety. The peace of God wants to be a protector or security guard over your heart and mind today!

The Peace of God is An Interagent

Not a familiar word, but 'interagent' means a mediator or umpire. Again, Apostle Paul writes in Colossians 3:15 "*And let the peace of God rule in your hearts, to which also you were called in one body; and be thankful.*" It is interesting that Paul wrote about peace to the Ephesian and Colossian believers while he himself was imprisoned. He experienced the peace of God in jail, and as you can see it had nothing to do with his situation or location. That is a good lesson for us, because when we are going through turbulent times our souls –emotions, intellect and will – want to dominate and dictate how we ought to feel and react. But Paul said *let* the Peace of God rule; it is a deliberate act of the will. Paul surely knew how to *let* the peace of God rule in his heart.

"Let the peace of God rule. . ." the word '*rule*' means to be an umpire, and is commonly used in reference to the Olympics and other games. It means 'to be a director, or mediator, or arbiter of public games; to preside over them and preserve order and to distribute the prizes

to the victors'. The meaning here is that the peace of God is to be to us what the governor at the games was to those who contended there. It is to preside over and govern the mind; to preserve everything in its place; and to save it from distress, anxiety, and perplexity. The key, however, is for us to *let* or allow peace to do its job, which is to preside or rule in our hearts.

Another thing is that the sports umpire watches the players to make sure that they are playing according to the rules. He usually has the last word as to whether a player is out or not. So when anxious thoughts and doubts come knocking at the door of your heart to gain entry, Paul says we are to allow or let the peace of God make a ruling or to make a decision.

As an interagent, the peace of God acts as a referee over your heart and mind, ruling in your favor that fears, doubt and anxious thoughts are not welcomed. Peace has the last word! And it says, "Worries, fears, anxiety, you are so out of here!"

The Peace of God is Abundant

2 Peter 1:2 *"Grace and peace be multiplied to you through the knowledge of God and of Jesus our Lord."* Multiplied means 'to increase, to abound.' The Amplified puts that verse this way, *"May grace (God's favor) and peace (which is perfect well-being, all necessary good, all spiritual prosperity, and freedom from fears and agitating passions and moral conflicts) be multiplied to you in [the full, personal, precise, and correct] knowledge of God and of Jesus our Lord."* So according to this verse, peace can be increased in measure to our full personal and correct knowledge of God and Jesus our Lord.

As we come to know Jesus better and better, our peace, that is our perfect well-being, our spiritual prosperity and freedom from fears and agitation of mind, freedom from moral conflicts, will be multiplied to us. You could actually put it in the form of an equation that reads like this - Increased and correct knowledge of God and Jesus Christ = Increased peace in your life. It is in knowing God and His Son Jesus more intimately that makes way for more of the peace of God to invade and fill our lives, while pushing out and evicting negative emotions. I pray God's peace be increased and abound in you today.

The God of Peace is Militant
Part 1

"And the God of peace (shalom) will crush (bruise) Satan under your feet shortly..." – Romans 16:20. First we talked about the peace of God, now it is the God of Peace. Peace or Shalom (Hebrew for peace) now takes on personality - it is Someone. God Himself shows up personally for us and we need to know He is serious about our peace and against anything or anyone who wants to rob us of it.

The God of peace gets right into the thick of things; the verse says He will bruise Satan under your feet shortly. The word 'bruise' means *'to break in pieces, to shatter, to cause to splinter into fragments.'* Now according to Romans 16:20, we are looking at the ultimate destructive power of peace. It is aggressive, it is militant – it will crush Satan or bruise him, shatter his works under our feet shortly.

Some of the meanings of shalom are *'completeness, prosperity, safety, contentment, healing, blessing and rest'.* However, the ancient

Hebrew spelling of *'shalom'* is interesting because it speaks only indirectly about the multiple meanings just mentioned, but it reveals something very profound that captures the essence of shalom. The Hebrew language is a pictorial language, something like Chinese, where the letters actually represent images. When you put the images or lettering together according to the ancient Hebrew spelling of *shalom,* the meaning reads "Destroying the authority that establishes chaos..." The God of peace – Shalom, takes the fight to yet another level.

The God of peace is militant and He will destroy any authority or power that creates chaos in our lives.

The God of Peace is Militant
Part 2

Now let's go back to our verse in Romans 16:20, *"And the God of peace (shalom) will crush (bruise) Satan under your feet shortly..."* Having learnt what 'to bruise' means in Romans 16:20, let's now look at the word 'shortly'. Shortly means *'quickly, speedily, in haste'* – the God of peace does not waste time about it. He, our Peace Personified, takes no prisoners where we are concerned. Whatever is a threat to our minds, to our spirits, our bodies, our dreams, our family, our destiny, He says He is going to shatter, break it, demolish it into pieces – and with haste under your feet! That is, He will give us dominion over the accuser and his agents who try to subvert our minds and destroy our peace.

God says, "You don't need to fight in this battle! You just rest in Me because I, the Prince of Peace, am taking care of it to see that you are fully restored and very quickly." This is a sure word of encouragement for someone. Peace is militant, He will confront your enemies; He is combatant, and is an opponent to all that comes against you!

They further disgraced the prisoners by stripping them naked for all to see; evidence that their enemies had lost their power. It was an ultimate show of conquest.

The Peace of God is Militant
Part 3

Follow me some more to see why this statement is so powerful. Speaking of Jesus, Colossians 2:15 from the Message Bible says, *"And having stripped all the spiritual tyrants in the universe of their sham authority at the Cross and marched them naked through the streets."* In ancient days, a conquering king and his army would parade their captive prisoners through the city streets to show off to the citizens that they had gained the victory over their enemies. What was more humiliating about this was how they did it. They further disgraced the prisoners by stripping them naked for all to see; evidence that their enemies had lost their power was. It was an ultimate show of conquest.

Jesus, through His death and burial, stripped Satan and his cohorts of all their authority. The NKJV says *"He made a public spectacle of them, triumphing over them in it."* But listen to this, the reason why Jesus Christ our Prince of Peace can boast that He has destroyed the imposter/the sham authority that establishes chaos in our lives, is because 2000 years ago He was brutally beaten, stripped, humiliated and paraded through the streets of Jerusalem while carrying the weight of His wooden cross. All this He suffered for our sakes.

Jesus took on Himself the ridicule and degradation that we deserved so that we do not have to be victims to chaos anymore. He paid the ultimate price with His life to break the hold of Satan on our lives. But He rose triumphantly from the grave and now He is the ultimate power and authority who deals with the roots of chaos in our lives.

Now the Prince of Peace has come to destroy the authority that dares to establish chaos in our lives. The Lord gets personally involved in all that would come to establish anarchy in our lives; all that would threaten to take away our peace of mind, want to take us to the edge of insanity, to rob us of our sleep, health, finances . . . our inheritance. The Militant God of Peace crushes Satan under our feet with haste. Glory to God! Hallelujah!!

The Peace of God is His Judgment in our Favor

In court cases you have the plaintiff – the one who makes the accusation, and the defendant – the one accused of the crime or injustice. When the judge has heard all the testimony related to the case, he/she makes a final ruling in favor of either the plaintiff or the defendant. In our case, God's judgment is in our favor; He has brought His gavel down ruling in our favor against the false accusations of the enemy. Peace it is – nothing missing nothing broken! It is a done deal! Isaiah 26:12 says *"LORD, You will establish peace for us, for You have also done all our works in us."* The KJV says *"The Lord will ordain peace for us."* The plaintiff, the accuser, Satan loses his case against us. The Lord's judgment, His decree in our favor is peace!

I don't have to guess, nor do I have to ask; I know that there are many of God's people who have been experiencing serious difficulties and anxieties of such proportions that you think that you will go insane. Actually, the enemy has been telling you that you will lose your mind. If he said it to me I know he has said it to you. But today I bring words of hope to encourage you – The LORD, will establish peace for you! It is His ruling in your favor against the accusations of the enemy.

We have learnt that God's peace is vigilant – it will watch over you, transcend all your finite thinking. It is a peace that is not of this world, it will reside in you, be present with you, it will rule out anxieties and fears, it will increase in you and it is God's judgment in your favor. The God of peace will crush or bruise Satan under your feet with immediate effect. He is the warrior God, the militant One, the One who fights for us - Hallelujah!

The Peace of God is His Announcement to the World

The announcement made by the angels to the shepherds regarding Jesus' birth, *"Glory to God in the highest, and on earth peace, goodwill toward men,"* was an announcement of peace, friendliness, friendship to the world. God is not mad at the world, He loves the world, and has expressed this in sending His Son Jesus Christ, the Prince of Peace, to earth, so that through His death and resurrection man can be reconciled back to God (John 3:16).

Why peace? Because the world is at war with God; sinners are at enmity with their Creator and against each other. But Jesus is God's mediator between Himself and man, *"For there is one God and one Mediator between God and men, the Man Christ Jesus"* – 1Timothy 2:5. And this is what He did, as Mediator He, *"... Offered himself in exchange for everyone held captive by sin, to set them all free"* – 1Timothy 2:6 The Message Bible.

The news is out – God's announcement of peace to the world is Jesus Christ; who came into the world to save sinners of whom I am chief, Apostle Paul said (1 Timothy 1:15)

The Call to Be Peacemakers

Do you know Jesus Christ as your Saviour and Lord? Then preach the good news; go everywhere and in every way announce the good news of peace. Romans 10:15 declares, *"And how shall they preach unless they are sent? As it is written: "how beautiful are the feet of those who preach the gospel of peace, who bring glad tidings of good things!"* Let the world know that God is not angry at them, He loves them, that is why He sent His Son to die for them (John 3:16)

If you don't know Jesus Christ as your Savior and Lord, then this is a superb opportunity to receive Him into your life and end the separation. Christ died so that you can be reconciled to the heavenly Father and finally experience His peace in your heart and mind. He is waiting! Shalom!

"Now may the God of peace Himself sanctify you completely; and may your whole spirit, soul, and body be preserved blameless at the coming of our Lord Jesus Christ"

– 1 Thessalonians 5:23

"Now the God of peace be with you all. Amen." – Romans 15:33

About the Author

Linda Jones is an ordained minister and pastors ***Walking on Water Teaching & Equipping Centre (WOWTEC)*** whose mission statement is *"Equipping you for life and ministry."* She also is the Founder and Director of – ***Women of Worth Ministries (WOW).*** She is a conference speaker and hosts workshops, seminars that address practical and relevant issues that affect both the spiritual, physical, emotional lives of women (as well as men). Her bimonthly radio program, ***Words of Wisdom,*** reaches out to the lost and those who have fallen away from the Lord. The focus is to direct them to the place and Person of healing and restoration, who is Jesus Christ.

Linda's personal mission statement is from Luke 4:18-19. She has a passion to see people, especially those in the Body of Christ, healed in every dimension of their lives. So that they can be thoroughly equipped in the Word and with life skills to go and fulfill the call of God on their lives, expand the kingdom of God in the earth and glorify Jesus Christ.

Linda holds a Bachelor of Theology from Christian International School of Theology, Santa Rosa California. She is a prolific writer and has authored several books, the most recent "Soul Survivor". She has conducted several productions, one entitled "Out of the Ashes" which is from her book by the same name.

Other Books by Linda P. Jones

Soul Survivor – *My Journey from trauma to triumph*, Linda's new and exciting biography.

Out of the Ashes – True stories of ancient women whose lives have been restored out of the ashes of loss, despair and failure to wholeness

What Aileth Thee? – The *Penetrating Question God Asks That Can Lead to Your Healing.* It is based on Genesis 21, the real life drama of Hagar and her son Ishmael. We learn from their experience how God lovingly invites us to be healed of our woundedness and fulfill His purpose for our lives

For This Child I Prayed – *A Practical Guide to Biblical Parenting.*

Great Gifts to Give Your Children – Introduces parents to a set of values they can give their children that shape their character and leave a rich legacy for generations. For example - Gifts of Prayer, Affirmation, The Blessing, Unconditional Love, Value of Money.

Daily Declaration for Kingdom Kids – a four-part devotional for children ages 4-15 years

Contact Information:

Email:

womenofworthbarbados@gmail.com or

iamasoulsurvivor@gmail.com

Website:

walkingonwatertec.org

Facebook pages:

http://www.facebook.com/pastorlindapjones

or

https://www.facebook.com/lpjoneswomenofworthministries

Made in the USA
San Bernardino,
CA